Please return book to:
Ms. Christianna Rennard

the
ZACCHAEUS
effect

CG

the Zacchaeus effect

Sometimes the only way

to refresh your relationship

with Jesus

is to go out on a limb

emil dean peeler

Foreword by Randy Maxwell

PACIFIC PRESS® PUBLISHING ASSOCIATION
Nampa, Idaho
Oshawa, Ontario, Canada
www.PacificPress.com

Designed by Michelle C. Petz

Copyright © 2004 by
Pacific Press® Publishing Association
Printed in United States of America
All Rights Reserved

Additional copies of this book are available by calling toll free 1-800-765-6955 or
visiting http://www.adventistbookcenter.com.

Library of Congress Cataloging-in-Publication Data

Peeler, Emil Dean, 1961-
The Zacchaeus effect : sometimes the only way to refresh your relationship with Jesus is to get
out on a limb / Emil Dean Peeler.
p. cm.
ISBN 0-8163-2050-0
1. Spiritual life—Seventh-day Adventists. 2. Zacchaeus (Biblical character) I. Title.

BV4501.3.P44 2004
248.4'867—dc22   2003069038

04 05 06 07 08 • 5 4 3 2 1

dedication

This book is dedicated to my parents, Arlie and Thomasina Peeler, who constantly give me the greatest gifts in the world: unconditional love, mind-boggling consistency, and total support. I am so thankful for being a piece of fruit that came from your tree.

acknowLedgments

I often say that if I had to describe myself in a single word, it would be *blessed*. From my earliest memories to the present, I can truly say that God has smiled on me.

Because of this I was moved to include this page to personally thank God and some of the people who have been influential in helping me to grow and develop as one of His children and who encouraged me in the writing of this book, for I believe this volume is but a combination of my experiences, influences, and divine inspiration.

To my wife Brenda: Your love, prayers, belief, insight, and inspiration helped me to focus during the times of delays and doubt.

LaDonna, Nicole, Alisha, (and Jeremiah): Your daddy is inspired to thank God every time I see you. You add so much joy in my life.

Barron (and Evelyn, Eryn, and Bryson), my brother and best friend: Your faithfulness, excellence, and unselfishness in your musical projects gave me a model of determination that I have employed to complete this volume.

Ivan Leigh Warden: It was you who planted the seed and encouragement for me to write while we worked together in the "urban war zone" of Los Angeles many years ago. It has taken a while, but now you can see and taste the fruit!

Dr. Audrey Howard: I praise God for your spending the time to carefully edit and comment on my early drafts. Though you didn't know it, your opinion was pivotal in my decision to ask God to move it forward. I respect you so much for your godly judgment and professionalism.

Randy Maxwell: Your kindness, insights, encouragement, and willingness to lead me through uncharted waters have given me a true picture of genuine Christianity. Simply put—though I tremendously respect you as one of my favorite authors, I have even more appreciation of you as God's man. Thanks so much for everything!

Dr. James Richard Doggette, Sr.: It was your awesome sermon on Zacchaeus more than twenty years ago while we were in seminary that captured my attention and set me on a quest to finding my own tree. An awesome concept! Much thanks!

Family and relatives who have helped to shape and encourage me: Grandma Peeler, Annie Files, Marcus Peeler, David Durley, Mary Jane Adams, Nelia Bell Haynes, Dexter Smith, Frances Norton, and all of the Files, Durley, and Peeler clans.

Preachers, mentors, and friends who have loved, taught, helped, and/or encouraged me throughout my life and ministry: Pastor J. Anthony Boger, Bronson and Dr. Gina Brown, Pastor Deon Chatman, Dr. E. E. Cleveland, Derek and Angel Cohill, Trinon and Dannielle Coleman, Dr. Craig A. Dossman Sr., Pastor Byron Dulan, Pastor Royal and Dominique Harrison, Pastor Cleveland Hobdy III, Pastor Martin L. Howard, Dr. Samuel R. Hutchins, Darrel A. and Pat Jackson, Dr. Craig Johnson, Dr. William Augustus Jones, Dr. Abraham Jules, Dr. George King, Pastor James G. Lee, Pastor EuGene Lewis, Pastor Alphonso McCarthy, Pastor Brian Neal, Pastor Warren J. Neal, Pastor J. J. Nortey, Pastor Terence O'Bryant, Dr. Jere Patzer, Pastor Lorenzo Paytee, Pastor Walter Pearson, Pastor Gerald Penick, Pastor George Rainey, Pastor David Richardson, Dr. Ron C. Smith, Pastor Allen Sovory, Pastor Randy Stafford, Gregory and

Rev. Penni Sweetenburg-Lee, Dr. David L. Taylor, Pastor Ray Turner, Dr. Ivan Williams, Dr. Jesse Wilson, Paavo and Jeri Wilson, Dwayne Witherspoon, and Pastor Marc K. Woodson.

Thanks to all the saints in the congregations that have allowed me to be a part of them over the years: Capitol City Seventh-day Adventist Church, Sacramento; Berean Seventh-day Adventist Church, Los Angeles; Compton Community Seventh-day Adventist Church; 16th Street Seventh-day Adventist Church, San Bernardino; and, presently, the Maranatha Seventh-day Adventist Church, San Diego (all in California).

And finally, to the staff of Pacific Press: Thank you for the opportunity to work together to build His kingdom.

God has used all of you and many others to make my life a blessed one.

EDP

contents

foreword

Do you believe that great things can come in small packages? You must, because you bought this book. Good choice. As you are about to find out, size is no measure of greatness.

Zacchaeus was a small man with a large problem. His life was a mess, and he knew it. People looked down on him—literally because of his height and figuratively because of his greed. The guilt and loneliness were becoming too much for him to bear.

Then one day this little man had a big idea. He would see Jesus, the miracle Man from Nazareth. However, Zacchaeus had high hopes but low prospects. The crowd around Jesus was too tall, and Zacchaeus was too small. What could he do?

Zacchaeus took a risk. He literally went out on a limb to make sure nothing would stand in the way between him and Jesus. What happened next changed his life forever. If you read the following pages with the same determination and desire that Zacchaeus had, you're sure to experience some big changes in your own life.

Emil Peeler has given us a quick and fun read. But that doesn't mean *The Zacchaeus Effect* is "lite" fare. The brevity of the book is what makes it pack such a wallop. With the skills of the anointed preacher he is, Emil takes a relatively brief incident from the life of Jesus and digs deep beneath the surface to unearth brilliant gems of truth to enrich our lives. The chapters, like Zacchaeus himself, are short. But the message in each one is huge.

Maybe you're feeling small and insignificant as you read these words. Maybe your problems or your sins seem so great that you're about to give up hope that God can—or even wants to—help you. Well, just as Jesus entered into Zacchaeus's personal space and forever altered his reality, He's about to do the same for you. Keep reading and come out a little farther on that limb with Zacchaeus. Take a risk. Jesus is passing by. Big changes are just ahead. This is your lucky day.

–Randy Maxwell

introduction

That winter night as I drove home, nearly blinded by the tears that welled up in my eyes, I began to count the blessings of my childhood, one by one. You see, earlier that evening as I was concluding a counseling session with one of the staff of a group-home facility, I noticed Lawrence in his room in an unusually sullen mood. I began to probe for the reason for his noticeably dejected spirit.

"Dr. P.," he said, "I'm having the worst day of my life. I can't believe that on my birthday I won't be able to do anything fun. Life sucks!"

Initially skeptical about the facts of his outburst, I soon learned that it was indeed his birthday. And indeed, no special plans or provisions were made for a celebration of any kind to mark his twelfth year of life.

Because he didn't have the privilege of being raised in a stable home environment, Lawrence became a ward of the court system when he was a very young child. He was first assigned to a foster family, and, after facing some difficulties, was placed in a group home. For nearly four years I, as his motivational therapist and friend, had the honor of watching him develop in this setting. Very short for his age, he was nonetheless bright, likeable, and plenty mischievous. Lawrence was a mixture of hormones, curiosity, and adolescence. Though we had our moments, I could honestly conclude that we had a pretty solid bond.

All that mattered now, though, was that on his "special" day nothing seemed so special. As he watched the sun sink low into the western hemisphere, his spirits sank even lower. Written all over his face were disappointment and anger.

Recognizing the obvious oversight, I told him to put on his shoes and jacket because I was going to take him out for his birthday. His eyes lit up. His smile returned. His sad countenance turned to joyful anticipation. All he could do was say, "Thanks, Dr. P.!"

A short drive later, we arrived at an amusement park that had a myriad of video games and virtual rides. To ensure he would have a great time, I purchased

Lawrence a ton of tokens so that he could have the run of the place. With his pockets spilling over with kids' gold, he asked, "What are *we* going to play first?" I was startled for a moment, but it soon dawned on me that my friend's primary need was not only to *go* some place special, but also to *share* the time with someone he believed to be special. He didn't want to celebrate his birthday all by himself. He desired a significant relationship with someone who liked being with him with no strings attached.

I didn't need much prodding to join in on the fun that evening, because truthfully, I'd secretly kept a few tokens for my own enjoyment. (Please don't laugh at me!) That night, because of his invitation, I turned into a big kid again. We played game after game. We laughed. We talked. We had fun! Actually, I don't know who was having more fun. After finishing the games, I took him to his favorite place to eat. On our way home I stopped to get him a birthday cake with his name on it to share with the other boys in the group home.

While walking back to the car, he looked up to me and said words that I didn't expect nor will I readily forget. "Dr. P., thank you so much for making my birthday the best day that I've ever had in my life! I never had a dad before, but at least I got to see what having a good dad is like. You're the greatest!"

An irrepressible smile crossed my face as I silently thanked God for using me to bring momentary happiness to a boy. I gave Lawrence a high five and, because I didn't know what to say, mumbled a few unintelligible words that I'm certain made no sense to my young friend. Lawrence's words, though, have echoed in my memory since the moment that he spoke them: *"At least I got to see what having a good dad is like!"*

While I have no reason to doubt the sincerity of his expressions of gratitude for the day's activities, I've nonetheless concluded that the reason for the depth of his appreciation stemmed from his intense yearning to be connected to a "good dad." I've studied for years about how the *absence* of a father figure can negatively impact on the lives of children. But on that evening, I specifically became aware of the value and the power of a good father who decides to be *present* in the lives of his children. For Lawrence, it took only one evening to get a glimpse of what a good father could mean to his life.

Your Father

This book is about a Father who earnestly seeks to be an integral part of your life. By looking through the lens of a biblical character named Zacchaeus, you will hopefully get a glimpse of what the presence of the ultimate "good Dad" can mean in your life. Let me be crystal clear before I move forward: I'm not speaking of your biological father or of the one who has raised you or is helping to raise you. I'm speaking of the One who really created you, the One who loves you with an inexplicable love; the One who desires to be with you forever!

Sadly, because of the presence of evil in this world, all humanity has been cruelly separated from our Father. Consequently, we're placed in the group homes of our existence and left to seek on our own for purpose, love, meaning, and acceptance. In our desperation we try anything and everything to attempt to fill the void that sin has caused. But, unbeknownst to the masses, what we're really longing for is to be connected to our heavenly Father. Yet the highway toward discovery of this ultimate relationship is often littered with bad choices, blighted dreams, and wasted years. The road is also filled with barriers, detours, and potholes that are intended to make us quit. The adversary's primary job is to keep us from knowing our true Father and having a relationship with Him.

On Zacchaeus's "rebirth day," he discovered, as we must, that it was God alone who planned and orchestrated the time and place for the greatest encounter of his life. It is God alone who comes into our homes to sort out all of our hurts, failures, and disappointments, to freely give us the gift of His freedom, forgiveness, and companionship through His Son. His encounters are divinely designed to counteract the mission of the enemy and to bring restoration and order to a broken family. His plans to reach us are intentional. We're never victims of fate, chance, or accidents. He wants his children back so badly that He literally has died for that privilege. All we have to do is accept His gift. *His ultimate present to us is His presence!*

Then, once you have received His gift, a beautiful relationship begins between Father and child, Creator and creature. A relationship in which there is a whole lot of talking, sharing, and even playing together! And the greatest benefit is that His presence isn't reserved for only a few hours on the day of your rebirth, but forever!

As we begin to study this day in the life of Zacchaeus, I sincerely hope that you, too, will get a snapshot of a Father who is planning to celebrate with you the party of your life. Go ahead, have some real fun for a change ... and watch your Father smile!

CHAPTER 1

tHe pLan

Jesus entered and passed through Jericho (Luke 19:1, KJV).

God has a plan for you—a divine scheme for your existence, a holy blueprint for your life. Not just for your family or your church or your country, but for you! You may not know, understand, or have accepted it, but He has it. It is intentional. Out of the billions of people who have lived and died on this earth, you've been chosen. *God* wants to be involved in a relationship with you.

I realize that this may be a bit much to swallow. The cynic in you may prefer to deny such a claim. But the fact of the matter remains: It's true. The Creator yearns for your friendship. Take the story of Zacchaeus, for example.

Before Jesus rose up that morning to spend quality time with His Father, Zacchaeus was already on His day planner, His agenda, His mind. Out of all His tasks and assignments for that particular day, our Savior's ultimate goal was to enter into a new relationship with someone whom He'd been preparing to meet for a long time—in fact, since his birth. Jesus' plan was to give Zacchaeus something that he couldn't earn, didn't deserve, and wouldn't comprehend: His grace, His unconditional love, and His peace. But most of all, Jesus desired to unveil the plans for his future. "Jesus entered and passed through Jericho" (Luke 19:1).

The way of Jesus often seems so subtle, almost inconspicuous. Yet here He is preparing to enter into Zacchaeus's personal space to change his life radically and positively. He was literally passing by just to see if this time He'd be noticed. He had so much more for Zacchaeus to experience and to know. Imagine the Creator of the universe taking the time to get to know you personally—up close, inside and out!

I once heard a preacher say, "In our present-day mind-set of skepticism and unbelief, many have unfortunately decided to accept the enemy's lies about God." Lies that say, "If God actually exists, His knowledge is severely limited. Therefore, He doesn't actually *know* about our situations, what we are facing or even how we are feeling." Lies that claim He's so involved in the massive agenda of the world that He doesn't have the time to focus on the unpleasant details of our puny lives.

The devil's next trick is to declare that if God actually does know about our present predicament, He doesn't *care* one way or another about what we are going through, that our problems are out of His hands and we are simply victims of fate, that God would never invest His feelings in creatures with such minor and petty concerns. And to crush all our hope, the father of lies will sway us to believe that even if God did know and care about us, He really doesn't have the *power* to change anything. He's a powerless, impotent deity. All glitter, no gold! All talk, no action! Then Satan will often drive his point home by making us look at all the injustice, suffering, and hurt in the lives of "innocent" people. If God really had the power, wouldn't He *do* something to fix up all the mess?

Something to Remember About God

All the members of my family are huge fans of the Los Angeles Lakers basketball team. Recently, my girls and I surprised my wife, Brenda, on Mother's Day by getting her playoff tickets to an important game against the San Antonio Spurs. (Before anyone questions my true motive in purchasing these tickets, let me assure you that she really *is* a bona fide, flag-waving, T-shirt wearing fan . . . honest!)

Anyway, it was an awesome game. The place was packed; the crowd (along with my wife) loudly cheered on their team. The game was extremely exciting; the score was very close. With about a minute remaining, the Lakers had taken a two-point lead and San Antonio had possession of the ball. The Lakers then stole the ball and scored a basket, to the delight of the crowd. The place erupted into utter pandemonium. There was dancing in the aisles.

The Spurs called a timeout to refocus and plan another play. I will probably never forget what I saw next. As I perused the crowd with my binoculars, I noticed two great Hall of Fame basketball players sitting next to each other across the way: Bill Russell and Kareem Abdul-Jabbar.

What captured my attention most was that their deportment was in stark contrast with that of us ordinary fans. Now, you have to get the picture of what was going on. The crowd was up on their feet. The place was electric. Everyone at Staples Center was standing, clapping, cheering, and hoping for a victory. But in the midst of all the noise and excitement, these two guys were just sitting, almost expressionless. I questioned in my mind, *How can they just sit there with so much energy in the building and, more importantly, when the game is on the line?*

Then it hit me. These two basketball giants weren't fans—they were *champions!* With seventeen championship titles and eight Most Valuable Player awards between them, they'd literally seen it all. In the world of professional basketball, there was very little that they hadn't experienced. They had probably gone through every emotion associated with victory and defeat. These two men had accomplished virtually everything that could be done on a basketball court.

Because of this, they were watching the game with a totally different perspective from the fans, and, for that matter, even from the players who were on the court. Like the rest of us in the crowd, they were enjoying the moment. But they were in control of their emotions because they had already—and many times—experienced the glory of victory.

Too often we who serve God forget that God is still on the throne and that He is in complete control. God is never surprised at the events that are happening to us or around us. He is never overwhelmed by bad news or caught off guard by a challenging ordeal. *He is God!* He is sovereign. That simply means He can do what He wants whenever He wants. He sees all. He knows all. He is everywhere all at the same time. And get this: Because He is righteous, He can never make a mistake. Everything He does is always at the right time. Because He is the ultimate Champion of love, His perspective is totally different than ours.

When the Jews were at the point in their journey where they were beginning to be convinced that God had forgotten all about them, He gave them reassurance with these words: "I know the thoughts that I think toward you, says the Lord, thoughts of peace and not of evil, to give you a future and a hope" (Jeremiah 29:11, NKJV). Simply put, God had not abandoned them, nor was He uninterested in the future of His people. God had a plan for them that involved a great future and plenty of bright hopes. He had neither forgotten them nor turned blasé toward their plight.

Zacchaeus may not have known it yet, but God was orchestrating the events of his day to include a significant encounter with His Son. He had a specific plan for Zacchaeus's future that wasn't an afterthought. God really is sovereign!

The best part is that there has never been a time when we haven't been on God's mind or thoughts! So, whatever you are facing this moment, comfort yourself by repeating over and over to yourself: "I'm on God's mind ... all the time!"

What's the difference between God and those two great players of bygone days? They can only watch and remember the past. God can still rule the court. Truth be told, He can't miss.

Swish!

(By the way, the Lakers won that day.)

the picture

Zacchaeus had it all. He possessed everything that was supposed to bring satisfaction. He had four things going for him: a favorable name, a recognizable title, lots of money, and above all, he was a man, which was a real advantage in that society.

The name *Zacchaeus* literally means "pure." During that time, one's name carried much more significance than it does today. His parents must have seen something special as they looked upon his cherubic face. "Zacchaeus!" Pure, undiluted, clean.

Zacchaeus also served as director of the IRS for the Roman government. He was the shrewd leader of this infamous department. He chaired the National Board of Tax Collectors, wrote policies, and hired and fired staff at will. Though tremendously popular, his reputation suffered because of the well-known corruption within the ranks. Just the mention of Mr. Z's name evoked strong responses. You either loved him or hated him.

Furthermore, this guy was super rich. It was no secret around town that he pocketed the excess taxes he ruthlessly charged the working class. He dressed in the best clothing, lived in the most posh neighborhood, ate the finest foods, and hired people to care for his every need. What a life!

You might say, however, that he was in vogue on the outside but vague on the inside. On this particular morning, he felt unfulfilled. Zacchaeus knew he needed something that would satisfy him. Though a man with "everything," he had a yearning for so much more.

From Riches to True Wealth

While vacationing in Canada years ago, Brenda and I and another couple were enjoying our meal at a restaurant when we noticed a couple staring at us. We smiled politely at them, but wondered why they were so interested in watching the events at our table.

Perhaps noticing our discomfort, the man, Mike, finally introduced himself and commented that there was something visibly different about us. He explained that it was a delight to see people having so much fun without the assistance of any alcoholic beverage. Then he boldly asked if we would join them for an evening of karaoke. Too embarrassed to admit that we didn't know what karaoke was, we said, "Sure." We arrived at the place where people who obviously had had a bit to drink were singing (now that was really funny!) on a small stage to prerecorded music.

In the middle of one of these performances, Mike began to pour out his soul to me. He was a successful businessman who'd made millions in real estate. He had all the trappings of success, but he was miserable: unfulfilled, empty, and depressed. Then he told me that he'd been asking people for several months what it was that he needed to make him happy ... but all the answers proved fruitless. Earlier he'd seen something in us that made him yearn for innocent joy. With a look of intensity, Mike asked if I could tell him why he still wasn't happy.

I quietly conveyed to him that what he was missing was peace of mind. In teary-eyed amazement, he leaned toward his wife and told her what I'd said. He'd been searching for something that could be found only in a relationship with God, and so that night, in the midst of blinding smoke and awful singing, I had the privilege of introducing my new friend to his heavenly Father.

After all the hype of having a recognizable name, an influential position, stunning power, and gobs of money, Zacchaeus, like Mike, still needed more. He called his assistant and informed her that he wouldn't be in the office for a while. He told her that he needed a little time for some soul searching. Before ending the conversation, Zacchaeus told her, "I don't know what it is about this Jesus guy, but I've got to meet Him. He's different, and I won't be back until I see Him for myself!" Little did Mr. Z know that he was the one who'd be found that day.

Reflecting on the WORD

Read and reflect on each text and try to determine the only way that humankind can have true purpose and peace.

"'Blessed are those who hunger and thirst for righteousness, for they shall be satisfied.'" —Matthew 5:6 (NAS)

"Trust in the LORD, and do good; dwell in the land, and feed on His faithfulness.

Delight yourself also in the LORD, and He shall give you the desires of your heart.

Commit your way to the LORD, trust also in Him, and He shall bring it to pass."

—Psalm 37:3-5 (NKJV)

"The kingdom of God is not a matter of eating and drinking, but of righteousness, peace and joy in the Holy Spirit, because anyone who serves Christ in this way is pleasing to God and approved by men. Let us therefore make every effort to do what leads to peace and to mutual edification." —Romans 14:17-19 (NIV)

"Jesus answered and said to her, 'Whoever drinks of this water will thirst again, but whoever drinks of the water that I shall give him will never thirst. But the water that I shall give him will become in him a fountain of water springing up into everlasting life.'"—John 4:13, 14 (NKJV)

" 'Thou dost keep him in perfect peace, whose mind is stayed on thee, because he trusts in thee. Trust in the Lord for ever, for the Lord God is an everlasting rock.'"
—Isaiah 26:3, 4 (RSV)

"The steps of a good man are ordered by the Lord, and He delights in his way."
—Psalm 37:23 (NKJV)

"Great peace have those who love Your law, and nothing causes them to stumble." —Psalm 119:165 (NKJV)

"For the wages of sin is death, but the gift of God is eternal life in Christ Jesus our Lord."—Romans 6:23 (NIV)

the problem—part 1

All Zacchaeus wanted was to observe Jesus in action in the flesh. He had heard so much about Him—incredibly amazing things. He was told that when Jesus touched the eyes of those who were blind, they could then see. He heard that through Jesus' ministry crippled individuals were now walking and that He restored sanity to people who had been mentally unstable. There even were stories circulating that He had restored some dead people to life. It seemed that all who had a personal encounter with this humble

Galilean left His presence positively impacted. Zacchaeus figured the odds were in his favor.

The morning was brisk as he poked around town, asking for the whereabouts of this Healer. Zacchaeus was lucky: Word was out that Jesus was going to be passing through Jericho that day. He noticed a group of people running by and muttering excitedly, "He's here!" Zacchaeus followed them, and to his surprise, when they finally got to the place where Jesus was teaching, there was already a massive crowd. The size of the crowd this common Man attracted was incredible—people were everywhere!

Zacchaeus tried to push his way through, but every time it seemed he was making progress, he was shoved to the back of the line. The Bible declares that Zacchaeus couldn't see Jesus because of the crowd. There were multitudes of people in the way of his encounter with the Master.

Whenever a sincere seeker decides to make an attempt to see Jesus, the devil will try to block it by using people. Over the years I've heard many reasons why people aren't interested in knowing God, and the predominant theme that echoes over and over again has to do with others. They'll say, "I would go to church but—" and then name one or two reasons like any of the following:

1. She cheated me, and she's supposed to be a leader in the church.

2. There are just too many hypocrites.

3. I saw the deacon at a questionable establishment with someone other than his wife.

4. Christians are no better than I am.

5. Every time I look around, another so-called Christian is getting in trouble.

6. The preacher isn't all that she's cracked up to be.

7. If he is what Christians are supposed to be all about, I don't want any of it!

Reality Check: No Perfect Humanoids!

He was probably one of the most gifted preachers that I've ever had the pleasure of hearing. Powerful. Dynamic. Dripping with charisma. Everywhere he traveled, crowds of people packed the halls, churches, and arenas to hear him preach the Word of God with clarity, accuracy, and rhythm. As a young preacher just beginning full-time ministry, I marveled at the way he moved crowds with such ease. I studied every aspect of his life and ministry that I could from a distance, and

I saw no flaws. Well-dressed and poised, he seemed to be a worthy model for me to emulate.

Imagine the shock and letdown I experienced when I learned that this preacher had been convicted of trafficking cocaine. He was a public success but a private failure. I could hardly believe my ears as the details of his shady side were exposed to a disappointed public. I found myself reeling from the disclosures and struggled even harder when asked to explain the apparent battle that raged in the soul of this preacher. What made it even worse was that I knew many people would use his failure as the reason they chose not get involved with Christianity. Even though he confessed to the people, served time for his conviction, and eventually returned to his church as a pastor, I couldn't help but wonder how this could happen to someone who appeared to be a great preacher and Christian.

Most of the time, what prevents people from seeing the Lord are the experiences they've had with the ones who are supposed to be the closest to Him. Zacchaeus learned a valuable lesson that day in Jericho. It was simple yet profound: When your goal is to see Jesus, try not to focus on the crowd!

Let me be clear. When one claims to be a born-again child of the King, he or she ought to live a life that is clearly distinguished from those who don't make this claim. Our lives should be living examples of honesty and grace. Our walk should always match our talk. I am grateful that I've been exposed to many consistently Christlike people. Yet the truth remains that there is no such thing as a perfect human specimen. The best of people falter and fall. All have weaknesses and blind spots. I constantly have to remind others who may admire the gifts (spiritual ones or otherwise) in me or in others to never fall into the trap of star-gazing. Remember, it's never safe to put flesh and blood on pedestals. Respect them, yes; deify them, never! Our only hope for improvement is to keep our focus on the Lord.

Zacchaeus could have chosen to throw in the towel and give up his goal to see the Galilean, Jesus. He could have convinced himself that at least he had put in a sincere effort. However, to his credit, he stubbornly continued forward with his plan. He figured that from all the reports he'd heard, seeing Jesus would be well worth the struggle.

Reflecting on the WORD

Read all the texts below and reflect on what our attitude should be when we are faced with trials and roadblocks from the enemy. Who is our confidence?

"Do not throw away your confidence, which has a great reward. For you have need of endurance, so that when you have done the will of God, you may receive what was promised." —Hebrews 10:35, 36 (NAS)

"We are hard pressed on every side, but not crushed; perplexed, but not in despair; persecuted, but not abandoned; struck down, but not destroyed.... Therefore we do not lose heart. Though outwardly we are wasting away, yet inwardly we are being renewed day by day.

For our light and momentary troubles are achieving for us an eternal glory that far outweighs them all. So we fix our eyes not on what is seen, but on what is unseen. For what is seen is temporary, but what is unseen is eternal." —2 Corinthians 4:8, 9, 16-18 (NIV)

"We are more than conquerors through him who loved us. For I am convinced that neither death nor life, neither angels nor demons, neither the present nor the future, nor any powers, neither height nor depth, nor anything else in all creation, will be able to separate us from the love of God that is in Christ Jesus our Lord." —Romans 8:37-39 (NIV)

"'When you pass through the waters, I will be with you; and when you pass through the rivers, they will not sweep over you. When you walk through the fire, you will not be burned; the flames will not set you ablaze.'" —Isaiah 43:2 (NIV)

"Be sober, be vigilant; because your adversary the devil walks about like a roaring lion, seeking whom he may devour. Resist him, steadfast in the faith, knowing that the same sufferings are experienced by your brotherhood in the world. But may the God of all grace, who called us to His eternal glory by Christ Jesus, after you have suffered a while, perfect, establish, strengthen, and settle you." —1 Peter 5:8-10 (NKJV)

CHAPTER 4

the problem—part 2

He sought to see Jesus who he was; and could not for the press,
because he was little of stature (Luke 19:3, KJV).

On a day filled with great expectations, Zacchaeus soon recognized that one's best plans are often met with hurdles and obstacles that delay progress. He wanted only to observe the Master in His own context, although perhaps he wanted to study new methods of mind control and survey the latest techniques of effective leadership. But the main reason he desired to see Jesus was to discover what made this Jew tick. It didn't appear that Jesus was interested in money or even clothes; for that matter, Zacchaeus had heard He didn't even own a house. Yet one couldn't keep from hearing about the inviting aura that surrounded His presence, an anointed charisma that was simply irresistible.

The massive crowd that stood in the way of Zacchaeus's encounter with Jesus was a definite problem—Satan will make sure that he uses people to prevent you from personally seeing the Savior. But there was also another problem for Zacchaeus. Not only were the people a hindrance, but he also had to recognize his own, ahem, *short*comings. Yes, he was short. He had to take responsibility for his own issues. For all the faults of the crowd, he could not pass the blame on them for his height.

I stand just under six feet three inches, and I've always felt pretty secure about my height. Yet a few years ago I literally bumped into basketball superstar Shaquille O'Neal of the Los Angeles Lakers. Not only did I feel like I'd run into a brick wall, but also, compared to him, I felt like a runt.

The Mistake of Measuring Ourselves by Others

Before we can see Jesus, we must recognize our own "shortness." It's not enough to complain about other people; we must see ourselves for who we really are. We may try to feel tall by putting on our titles or by showing off our "things." We may even attempt to make ourselves look tall by measuring ourselves next to those persons we've deemed to be of a lower status, either educationally, sociologically, racially, or even spiritually. Yet, in reality, no matter what we may think ourselves to be, we are all prodigals trying to find our way back home.

If we spent enough time searching the globe, we might all find someone we could feel superior standing next to. However, when it comes down to comparing ourselves to Jesus, there is no one who can match His height. Compared to His Majesty, we have all come up short! Romans 3:23 states clearly, "All have sinned, and come short of the glory of God" (KJV). That means everyone. Every politician, preacher, peasant, or parent. Every actor, athlete, artist, or adolescent. It doesn't matter the sphere of your influence or the size of your bank account. If you have come to this earth by way of birth, you've been infected with a disease called sin, which is the condition that causes humanity to be separated from our heavenly Father. It's that natural state of being that we are born with.

The fact is, humanity is more prone to have a short temper and a selfish nature than to be kind and giving. It's easier for us to lie than to tell the truth. It's more common for us to take the credit rather than to share the spotlight. It's literally "second nature" for us to talk of others' failings rather than deal with our own weaknesses. If you doubt this fact, let me ask a question: Can you name a person who had to procure lessons to learn how to sin? The answer is clear: There is no one.

Regardless of our backgrounds, color, jobs, or degrees, we are all on equal ground when it comes to our original status: SINNER! I was born a sinner. And make no mistake about your condition at birth: SINNER! Therefore, no one has any bragging rights because essentially our conditions are the same: SINNER! "*All* have sinned, and come short …"!

Now, let me hasten to write that we all have been given the power to choose whether or not to remain sinners. The good news of the gospel is that we do not have to stay the way we are. But on the road to meeting the Master we must be cognizant of one of the cleverest ploys of the devil: He tries to give people a false sense of security regarding their own righteousness by tempting them to turn their focus away from themselves and toward others. This raises the biggest hurdle to our quest to seeing the Lord.

Zacchaeus learned something that day—a lesson

that bears repeating time and time again. The greatest obstacle on the way to seeing Jesus is likely the person you face each day in the mirror. There'll always be people in the gallery of our lives who will try to make us stumble or block our path or simply get in our way. But the truth is that the greatest enemy we'll ever face is the enemy of self. An old song I remember singing as a child puts it more succinctly:

"It's not my mother or my father
But it's me, oh Lord, standing in the need of prayer!
It's not the preacher or the teacher
But it's me, oh Lord, standing in the need of prayer!"

Mark this down. The sooner we stop pointing our finger at other people's faults, failures, or limitations and begin to recognize just how much our own spiritual status lacks, the sooner we will be on our way to a personal encounter with the Savior. That's gospel. Anything else is simply being ... shortsighted!

Reflecting on the WORD

Read and reflect on each text, and determine the degree to which God desires to save us and to have us recognize the power we have over the enemy if we remain faithful and committed to Him.

"The Lord is not slow in keeping his promise, as some understand slowness. He is patient with you, not wanting anyone to perish, but everyone to come to repentance." —2 Peter 3:9 (NIV)

"We know that in all things God works for the good of those who love him, who have been called according to his purpose." —Romans 8:28 (NIV)

"Beloved, believe not every spirit, but try the spirits whether they are of God: because many false prophets are gone out into the world. Hereby know ye the Spirit of God: Every spirit that confesseth that Jesus Christ is come in the flesh is of God: And every spirit that confesseth not that Jesus Christ is come in the flesh is not of God: and this is that spirit of antichrist, whereof ye have heard that it should come; and even now already is it in the world. Ye are of God, little children, and have overcome them: because greater is he that is in you, than he that is in the world." —1 John 4:1-4 (KJV)

"Submit yourselves, then, to God. Resist the devil, and he will flee from you." —James 4:7 (NIV)

"The Lord is my light and my salvation—whom shall I fear? The Lord is the stronghold of my life—of whom shall I be afraid? When evil men advance against me to devour my flesh, when my enemies and my foes attack me, they will stumble and fall. Though an army besiege me, my heart will not fear; though war break out against me, even then will I be confident. One thing I ask of the Lord, this is what I seek: that I may dwell in the house of the Lord all the days of my life, to gaze upon the beauty of the Lord and to seek him in his temple. For in the day of trouble he will keep me safe in his dwelling; he will hide me in the shelter of his tabernacle and set me high upon a rock." —Psalm 27:1-5 (NIV)

" 'The eyes of the Lord are on the righteous, and His ears are open to their prayers; but the face of the Lord is against those who do evil.' And who is he who will harm you if you become followers of what is good?" —1 Peter 3:12, 13 (NKJV)

CHAPTER 5

the passion

He ran before, and climbed up into a sycomore tree to see him
(Luke 19:4, KJV).

One of the characteristics that separates ordinary people from extraordinary people is the spirit of passion: that sense of inner drive and purpose, the ability to stay focused and on target with a dogged tenacity. It's the "thing" that you have when you are doing something you believe you were born to do, the sense of urgency that makes you move forward when all the signs are pointing backward.

Zacchaeus was on a mission. Nothing and nobody was going to stop him from seeing Jesus—not the people who blocked his path nor the circumstances that faced him nor the obstacles that threatened to discourage him. No more excuses! No more playing the blame game or saying, "I'm too tired," "I'm too busy," "I've made too many mistakes in the past," or "I'm not smart enough!" Zacchaeus looked life squarely in the face and concluded that it was now or never. "Today I'm going to start over, and it'll begin by spending a few moments with this itinerant Preacher from Galilee!"

But consider this: Whenever we begin to focus on making decisions that will help change our lives positively, the enemy will emerge with weapons that impede our progress—like excuses, procrastination, apathy, and friends who'll throw water on our fire and put roadblocks in our path. If we let these weapons penetrate our mentality, we'll give the enemy the advantage even before the battle begins. And before we realize it, time and opportunity pass us by because we've allowed these weapons to destroy our passion to advance. I'm inspired by what Zacchaeus did next to accomplish his purpose.

And He Ran Before [the Crowd]

He moved as fast as he could away from the place that limited his vantage point. He didn't stick around to see if he was going to grow anymore. He didn't wait for someone to hoist him up. He didn't take time to try to convince the other people in the crowd to move so that he could see. He got on with it. He wouldn't accept no for an answer. He ran ahead of the crowd. That's passion!

In those days it wasn't proper for people of status to run in public—it was just not a dignified thing to do. Yet I believe there ought to be something in our lives we're so passionate about, something that so right- eously moves and inspires us that we're willing to risk losing our reputations, friendships, and even our lives to fulfill. Simply put, whenever we get serious about our pursuit of righteousness, we'll be faced with the definite reality of leaving some things—and some people—behind.

There are at least two realities to remember on our way to our eternal destiny: First, life will always be meaningless without a passion for God. The quest for meaning can never be satisfied by the pursuit of plea- sure and material possessions. Fame, power, sex, and money are all empty substitutes the devil uses as traps to deter us from seeking what we all long for. As a matter of fact, there's a need innate to all of humanity that only God can fill.

Take the time to ask yourself: What am I passionate about? Am I spending my time and energy on things that are lasting and permanent? Is God number one on my list of priorities? We would do well to look at David's passion as he wrote about his pursuit of God: "As the deer pants for streams of water, so my soul pants for you, O God. My soul thirsts for God, for the living God" (Psalm 42:1, 2, NIV).

The second thing you need to remember is that you'll never get to where you need to be if you choose to remain where you are. Are you tired of your present plight or circumstances? Have you bottomed out? Are you stuck in a rut? Wherever you are at this moment, one thing is clear: You'll never move forward while you're committed to standing still. Read that last statement again slowly and let it simmer for a moment.

After you're done contemplating that idea, get up and start moving! Before you know it, you'll be ahead of the pack.

Reflecting on the WORD

Read and reflect on each text below, and determine the role of faith in one's pursuit of God and godliness.

"Without faith it is impossible to please God, because anyone who comes to him must believe that he exists and that he rewards those who earnestly seek him." —Hebrews 11:6 (NIV)

"Be watchful, stand firm in your faith, be courageous, be strong." —1 Corinthians 16:13 (RSV)

"In it the righteousness of God is revealed from faith to faith; as it is written, 'But the righteous [person] shall live by faith.'" —Romans 1:17 (NAS)

"As you excel in everything—in faith, in utterance, in knowledge, in all earnestness, and in your love for us—see that you excel in this gracious work also." —2 Corinthians 8:7 (RSV)

"I can do all things through Christ who strengthens me." —Philippians 4:13 (NKJV)

"I say, through the grace given to me, to everyone who is among you, not to think of himself more highly than he ought to think, but to think soberly, as God has dealt to each one a measure of faith." —Romans 12:3 (NKJV)

"Therein is the righteousness of God revealed from faith to faith: as it is written, The just shall live by faith." —Romans 1:17 (KJV)

"Jesus answered and said to them, 'Have faith in God. For assuredly, I say to you, whoever says to this mountain, "Be removed and be cast into the sea," and does not doubt in his heart, but believes that those things he says will come to pass, he will have whatever he says.'" —Mark 11:22, 23 (NKJV)

the place

He ... climbed up into a sycomore tree to see him: for he was to pass that way. And when Jesus came to the place, he looked up, and saw him (Luke 19:4, 5).

One of the unforgettable scenes in the movie *Forrest Gump* pictures the lead character, Forrest, running without leg braces. Earlier in his life he'd been hampered by a disability that made it difficult for him to walk. But through hard work and determination, he overcame his obstacle and was set free, no longer hindered. And so he chose to run nearly everywhere he went.

On a day when a major disappointment had severely crushed his spirit, Forrest decided to handle his grief by running. So he ran ... and ran ... and ran. As he ran, people began to follow him: through fields and towns, down back roads and highways. He ran for what seemed to be weeks. Then, out of the blue, just as suddenly as he began, he stopped. The followers didn't understand. But it had dawned on Forrest, in spite of his zeal, passion, and dedication to running, that running could be pretty meaningless without a destination.

All too often life loses its meaning because many of us are running fast but headed nowhere. We're in motion without a destiny, spinning our wheels day in and day out: full calendars, work, home, bills, and family problems. Occasionally, we find time to laugh, but then it's back to the old routine. We've never been busier, but what really is the point of it all? Where are we headed? What's our destination?

In contrast to many of us, when Zacchaeus grew weary of a meaningless and empty existence, he determined to change his plight. Not only did he decide to run ahead of the crowd, but he did so with a noble goal in mind—to see Jesus for himself. And Zacchaeus reasoned that the best possible way to meet Him was to go to a place where He was scheduled to go by.

Zacchaeus Found His Tree

"He ... climbed up into a sycamore tree to see him: for he was to pass that way." Zacchaeus stopped running long enough to find a tree that would suit his needs. Being a short man, he needed a tree that had low branches so he could climb up without any help. As he searched, he discovered a sycamore tree that was growing right on the main road. He climbed up the tree, and then he did what is so difficult for many of us to do in this fast-paced, microwave society: He waited.

If our ultimate goal is to have a close encounter with the King of kings, we must learn two lessons from Zacchaeus's account. First, we must *stay focused on the goal!* We must not let the good things that we do keep us from doing the main things that are absolutely necessary to establishing a one-on-one relationship with God! I've discovered that we can get so busy doing the work of the Lord that we neglect getting to know the Lord of the work. God has to remind me constantly that His desire to know me is much more profound than His desire to know what I've done (or am doing) for Him.

Several years ago, I was cruising along in ministry. Though far from being a model pastor, I felt, at the very least, that I was a competent one. The church was growing and was beginning to make inroads into our community; finances were coming in, and I was receiving invitations to share my preaching gifts all over the country. Because of this, I was asked to serve on several boards and committees to address the needs of the constituency. To top it off, I was twice given the Pastor of the Year Award presented annually to the pastor with the most "success" in our region within our denomination.

To tell the truth, I was always busy—running from meeting to meeting, studying for sermons, visiting the sick, burying the dead. But in the midst of all my activity, God had to teach me a thing or two. Now, don't get me wrong: I can honestly say that I'd been careful to remain humble and to give God all the glory for any of the so-called success I was enjoying. My honest desire was to be a good minister (though it was the last profession I would have chosen on my own).

I'll never forget the shock I felt while driving down the road from my house when I distinctly heard God's voice calling me a failure and telling me how He desired to take me to another level. Although I can recall only hearing that voice in my life one other time, it was clear, distinct, and unmistakable.

I couldn't believe what I was hearing. Could God call me an imperfect minister? Absolutely! A failure? No way!

My immediate response to His verbal promptings was to be angry and defensive. I began telling Him that I hadn't chosen the ministry and if it wasn't for His interference in my "plans," then we wouldn't even be having this conversation. I then began sharing with Him my schedule, my baptismal record, my awards, and on and on about my "success." I reasoned, *How could He want more of me when I've given the best I could to the ministry?*

After all of my ranting, God spoke again. *"Emil,"* He softly said, *"you're indeed a good minister, but you have it all confused. Yes, I notice that you're working hard and staying busy for the sake of ministry. But you must understand that I don't want your ministry—I want YOU! Your ministry is only to be an overflow of the relationship that you've developed while getting to know Me!"* God was calling me into a greater intimacy with Him. I was spending most of my time working for Him instead of using it to get to know Him.

I constantly pray that I'll never forget the lesson God taught me that day. Yet, even during those moments when I get forgetful and start giving God's work greater priority than I give Him, He will always allow something (a burden, pain, trial, etc.) to enter my life to remind me to get back on track. The truth is, if all of our activity is not rooted in a passionate desire to get to know Jesus or an outgrowth of a heart overflowing with love for Him, we'll soon burn out, give up, or eventually stop running!

This is the second and probably the most important point for us to remember. We have places to put everything—our TVs, computers, food, cars, clothes, books, pets, and even our keys (though as I get older, I'm forgetting where I put those elusive little items!). And we know where certain things will go or won't go. For instance, we have determined that our car's proper parking place probably will not be in our living room but in the garage. Likewise, in our quest to encounter God, we must prioritize the place where we intend to convene with Him. We need to find a particular "tree" that helps us to see Him—a regular rallying spot with the Divine, a place where we can get a better vantage point, a private spot where we can be alone with God. We need to stop running long enough to begin to look for a place where we can begin our communication with Jesus.

Our "tree" may be the office, the bedroom, a quiet corner in the kitchen, or maybe the street where we walk early in the morning. Wherever we choose, we must go to that place regularly. We must make a daily climb up that tree! Remember this too: Sometimes while sitting on a branch, we may have to linger a while before He comes along. Yet I've discovered that Jesus always comes at the right time.

Before long, climbing trees will make us feel like children again—or better still, His child again!

Reflecting on the WORD

Read and reflect on each text to discover the beauty and benefits of open and regular communion with God.

" 'But when you pray, go into your room, close the door and pray to your Father, who is unseen. Then your Father, who sees what is done in secret, will reward you. And when you pray, do not keep on babbling like pagans, for they think they will be heard because of their many words. Do not be like them, for your Father knows what you need before you ask him.' " —Matthew 6:6-8 (NIV)

" 'Abide in Me, and I in you. As the branch cannot bear fruit of itself, unless it abides in the vine, neither can you, unless you abide in Me. I am the vine, you are the branches. He who abides in Me, and I in him, bears much fruit; for without Me you can do nothing. If anyone does not abide in Me, he is cast out as a branch and is withered; and they gather them and throw them into the fire, and they are burned. If you abide in Me, and My words abide in you, you will ask what you desire, and it shall be done for you.' " — John 15:4-7 (NKJV)

"Jesus answered and said to him, 'If anyone loves Me, he will keep My word; and My Father will love him, and We will come to him and make Our home with him.' " —John 14:23 (NKJV)

"It is good for me to draw near to God; I have put my trust in the Lord GOD, that I may declare all Your works." —Psalm 73:28 (NKJV)

"He that dwelleth in the secret place of the most High shall abide under the shadow of the Almighty. I will say of the LORD, He is my refuge and my fortress: my God; in him will I trust." —Psalm 91:1, 2 (KJV)

"Let us therefore draw near with confidence to the throne of grace, that we may receive mercy and may find grace to help in time of need." —Hebrews 4:16 (NAS)

"The Lord is near to all who call upon Him, to all who call upon Him in truth. He will fulfill the desire of those who fear Him; He will also hear their cry and will save them." —Psalm 145:18, 19 (NAS)

"'Look! I have been standing at the door, and I am constantly knocking. If anyone hears me calling him and opens the door, I will come in and fellowship with him and he with me.'" —Revelation 3:20 (TLB)

CHAPTER 7

the pronouncement

When Jesus came to the place, he looked up, and saw him, and said unto him, Zacchaeus, make haste, and come down; for to day I must abide at thy house (Luke 19:5, KJV).

I don't know how long Zacchaeus waited in that tree, but I can be pretty certain that it must have seemed like forever. Sometimes it's the waiting that can be most unbearable: the final hour of a flight that is going home after a long and taxing business trip; a test result; the third and final job interview; the wait for that last shot attempt, or field goal, or final pitch. Waiting, actually, can be almost as unnerving as the result.

A lump formed in Zacchaeus's throat as he saw the approaching crowd. From a distance he observed the slow-moving throng coming closer and closer. Beads of sweat began to form on his receding brow. As the mass arrived at the place where he was perched, the strangest thing happened: Jesus looked up at him! Imagine that—the Creator of the universe looking up at Zacchaeus. For so long he had been taunted and teased about how short he was. But now he felt a surge of pride because of the way that "look" made him feel—more satisfied than any amount of money ever did.

The "look" would have been enough for Zacchaeus. But Jesus actually knew him by name. And to top it off, the Lord had a personal message for him. Jesus said, "Zacchaeus, come down immediately. I must stay at your house today."

The Importance of Divine Encounters

Jesus was telling Zacchaeus that this was his moment for an ultimate divine encounter. It was do or die, sink or swim. It is the moment that comes to every person—the moment to decide to remain on the "lofty heights" of self-reliance or to move on to the stable ground of peace and love. Whatever is empty inside of you, the I AM is here to fill the void.

Don't miss the urgency of the message. Jesus emphasized the value and the importance of "today" and "now." So many of us have missed our assigned blessing because of a spirit of procrastination or a mind-set that has refused to seize the moment. One of the biggest lies we tell ourselves is that we have plenty of time. Therefore, we reason, it's no big deal if we squander massive amounts of time unwisely on things that have no eternal significance. The devil will trick us into believing that tomorrow is the better time to deal with such issues. The result of such thinking is often missed opportunities and regret. But the saddest part is that no matter how hard we try, we can never turn back the clock.

I remember hearing the story of a prisoner who sat on death row for a crime he committed when he was young and out of control. After several failed attempts to appeal his case, he fell into deep depression and refused to speak to anyone. Isolated and bitter, he came to accept his fate of execution by lethal injection.

He had already served nearly thirty years for the crime and for the greater portion of his sentence had been a model inmate. However, the pain of being rejected time and time again made him lose all hope. As a last ditch effort, his attorneys forwarded his case to the governor of the state to request a pardon. To his legal team's surprise, the governor granted the request after reviewing the case. The governor's only condition was that he be the one to deliver the news of the pardon.

Entering the prison the day before the scheduled execution, the governor, not wanting any undue attention, came dressed in a priest's attire. He was carrying the pardon with the name of the prisoner on it. Out of the corner of his eye, the prisoner saw the man dressed as a priest. Deciding that he did not want to hear anything God had to say, he refused to receive the visitor. Three times the man begged the prisoner to see him, and three times the prisoner told him to go away.

Finally, with tears in his eyes, the governor left the prison and rescinded the pardon. He recognized that he could not force anyone to receive his offer. After the governor departed, the prisoner was told about his guest. He cried and cried for the governor to return, but it was too late. Tragically, the man was executed the next day because he had blown his opportunity to gain unconditional freedom. He was so swamped in depression and bitterness that he missed his only chance for survival.

Zacchaeus had enough wisdom to recognize that yesterday is only a memory and tomorrow is not guaranteed. He also realized that the emptiness that he was experiencing was about to be filled—filled right now, in fact, and by a Person whose desire is not to be a temporary guest but who has boldly announced His plan to be a permanent resident: "I must stay at your house today!" Truly, this is salvation in a nutshell: Jesus coming by to fill up empty houses with His presence.

Whenever a person decides to establish and prioritize a place for a divine encounter, at least three things will happen. First, Jesus will meet you there. Period. Not "maybe" or "sometimes." He *will* come at precisely the moment that He has established for you before the world began.

Second, Jesus will know who you are and will call you by your name. You must always remember that you were created on purpose and for a purpose. You are more than what people have labeled you—you are His child, and He knows and loves *you!*

Finally, Jesus will offer you the greatest gift—His eternal presence. Years ago, the popular gospel group The Winans recorded a song entitled "Tomorrow" that is both timeless and relevant. It speaks of the urgency of receiving the Lord into your life when you have the opportunity: "Jesus says, 'Here I stand, won't you please take my hand?' And you say, 'I will ... tomorrow!'"

But, as the song says, "tomorrow is not promised," you'd better choose the Lord today "because tomorrow may very well be too late!"

Zacchaeus did not delay, and guess what? He received the gift of eternity. The best part is, so can you!

Reflecting on the WORD

Read and reflect on each text to understand the magnitude of God's redemptive grace and complete forgiveness.

"Blessed be the God and Father of our Lord Jesus Christ, who has blessed us with every spiritual blessing in the heavenly places in Christ, just as He chose us in Him before the foundation of the world, that we should be holy and without blame before Him in love, having predestined us to adoption as sons by Jesus Christ to Himself, according to the good pleasure of His will, to the praise of the glory of His grace, by which He has made us accepted in the Beloved. In Him we have redemption through His blood, the forgiveness of sins, according to the riches of His grace." —Ephesians 1:3-7 (NKJV)

"See how very much our heavenly Father loves us, for he allows us to be called his children—think of it—and we really are! But since most people don't know God, naturally they don't understand that we are his children. Yes, dear friends, we are already God's children, right now, and we can't even imagine what it is going to be like later on. But we do know this, that when he comes we will be like him, as a result of seeing him as he really is." —1 John 3:1, 2 (TLB)

"Let the wicked forsake his way and the evil man his thoughts. Let him turn to the Lord, and he will have mercy on him, and to our God, for he will freely pardon." —Isaiah 55:7 (NIV)

"The wages of sin is death, but the gift of God is

eternal life in Christ Jesus our Lord." —Romans 6:23 (NIV)

" 'The Son of Man has come to seek and to save that which was lost.' " —Luke 19:10 (NKJV)

CHAPTER 8

the pardon

Zacchaeus, make haste, and come down; for to day I must abide at thy house. And he made haste, and came down, and received him joyfully (Luke 19:5, 6).

A person's faith cannot be determined by what he or she says or feels. Furthermore, true faith cannot even be determined by what a person thinks or believes. The quality of a person's faith is determined by one thing and one thing only: obedience—by *doing* whatever God says to do, even if His instructions do not make sense at the moment.

Zacchaeus received the Lord's favor because he was willing to obey Him. Notice that when the Lord told Zacchaeus to get down out of the tree, Zacchaeus didn't waste any time asking questions or analyzing the possibilities. He simply did what Jesus asked him to do. He obeyed the Lord swiftly, completely, and joyfully. He came down from the tree and received a pardon: a clean slate, a second chance, instant salvation. The best word for this is *grace*. Zacchaeus was granted something that he did not earn, could not buy, and could not comprehend.

In addition to the grace he received, the moment that Zacchaeus said Yes to the Lord and followed His directives, something else was immediately given to him that made his life worth living. He received *joy*—God's great joy that comes only from being forgiven and restored back into a relationship with Him.

Let me make it clear: The joy that Zacchaeus received was not some lighthearted giddiness that gave him goose bumps. It was not even a feeling of happiness. It was much deeper than that. Happiness is always contingent on things and circumstances, so when they are present in our personal realm, we can be happy.

True joy is much different from mere happiness. Joy is a fruit of the Spirit. It isn't based on "because of" but rather on "in spite of"—it is that inner peace and unshakeable principle that arises from believing that one's value doesn't come from possessions or from people. It is that *gift* that makes you smile in the midst of your pain. It is that *thing* that gives you the certainty of God's presence even when all around you the walls are collapsing. No wonder the Bible exclaims, "The joy of the Lord is our strength," and that "weeping may endure for a night, but joy comes in the morning."

At some point during his descent from the tree to the ground, God granted Zacchaeus His joy. The Bible says, "He [Zacchaeus] … received him [Jesus] joyfully." Never forget that the road to joy always begins with obedience.

As I sit at my desk reflecting on this scene in the life of Zacchaeus, I can't help but think of how God— regularly and often—showers me with His grace and the joy that I have because of it. I shudder to think of how different things could have been without His mercy. I can truly understand the joy of being fully forgiven, but to end my testimony with that declaration would be giving just half the story.

The whole truth of the matter is that I can also relate to what it feels like to exist without any true joy— the times when I have rebelled and disobeyed and followed my own will. Yes, I also know the reality of living a life of emptiness, trying to fill my time and life with stuff that lasts for but a moment. But thank God, His grace always persists.

At age fifteen, I had a classic case of "stupid." Maybe I wasn't all that unique, but looking back, I believe that there were certain times when heaven had to work overtime on my behalf. I remember my father granting me permission to spend some time with two of my buddies. Of course, to say that seeing my friends was my true motive would not be telling the whole truth. First of all, one of my friends had just gotten his first car. Second, we had a serious crush on three sisters who lived with their family in the mountains about an hour's drive from where we lived. So, unbeknownst to my father, and (*gulp*) being the real "men" we were, we masterminded a perfect plan to take a drive and visit these girls.

As we traveled up the winding roads in the hills of Northern California, we laughed and listened to each other's foolery while music blared in the background. Though my actions didn't show it, I do recall feeling a bit uncomfortable about being deceitful to my father. Deep inside I knew I had made a mistake.

Let me pause here to tell you something we all need to know. It is always Satan's strategy to lure us into choices that will separate us from the Father's perfect plan and will for our lives. Satan constantly attempts to deceive us into thinking that we know what's best for our lives. He tries to convince us that we are wise enough or that we have enough education to be the "masters of our own fate." Not so; *any* road without God will ultimately lead to disappointment, dismay, and destruction.

Now back to the story: While cruising up the mountain, we took a wrong turn, and, before we knew it, we were lost. As we frantically sought to find our way, my teenage friend (and driving sensation) sped around a corner, only to face a narrow, one-lane bridge. On the other side of the bridge was a huge truck speeding toward us. Both vehicles were going too fast to stop, and there was no space to pull over to let the other one pass by. The reality facing us was that a head-on collision was imminent.

My short life raced before my eyes. Then, suddenly, out of fear and desperation, we called out the name of the Lord. I must admit that at the time I didn't comprehend all the significance associated with the wonderful name of Jesus, but on that day I discovered there *is* power in His name.

I wish I could describe what happened next, but I can't. The only thing we knew is that at one moment we faced certain death and the next moment we were on the other side of the truck, still traveling forward. No accident. No bruises. No explanation of how we were spared.

More than twenty-five years have passed since that day, and I still don't fully know how we made it through. However, I have no doubt in my mind as to *who* brought us through. Even in the midst of our foolishness, God heard our cry. And not only did He hear us, He saved us. Period. It was truly a miracle of grace and divine intervention. While the devil was initiating a plan for our destruction, God was activating a plan for our deliverance. The greatest news in the world is that God's love is so powerful that even in the midst of wrong turns, bad choices, and ill-advised journeys into dangerous territories, He is always there to protect us, forgive us, and to put us back on the righteous road of peace and joy.

Heaven's Hit List

Whenever God chooses the crucial moments of our lives to reveal Himself and show His awesome love and abiding presence, many of us make the mistake of believing that we are the ones who "found God." The truth is, He was never lost—we were. Every moment since our birth we have been on Heaven's hit list. God's love for us is limitless—He keeps pursuing us and orchestrating the events of our lives to place us where we will be able to recognize His voice. And then, once we've heard His invitation to us, He gives us the choice to accept or reject His offer of love. I like to call it "divine initiative"—that is, *He* is the One who is actively seeking *us*.

I believe that someone reading these words is hearing the Savior's call to "come down" from the unstable place that keeps you from knowing Him. He may be calling you down from a nagging habit that has bound you. He may be calling you down from a ragged past that keeps you in a constant state of guilt. He may be calling you down from an empty life of joyless amusement. He may even be calling you down from a relationship that you have prioritized over God. Whatever you have set up as your "place" of false refuge, it is time to come down and meet the real deal. It's time for you to allow the Lord to restore the joy.

Let me caution you. Once you decide to trust Him enough to obey Him, He will literally come in and totally renovate your house. But really, if the King is going to live there, nothing but the best will do.

Reflecting on the WORD

Read and reflect on each text to discover the role and value of obedience to God once one has been pardoned and cleansed.

"I urge you, brothers, in view of God's mercy, to offer your bodies as living sacrifices, holy and pleasing to God—this is your spiritual act of worship. Do not conform any longer to the pattern of this world, but be transformed by the renewing of your mind. Then you will be able to test and approve what God's will is—his good, pleasing and perfect will." —Romans 12:1, 2 (NIV)

"'No one can serve two masters. Either he will hate the one and love the other, or he will be devoted to the one and despise the other. You cannot serve both God and Money.'" —Matthew 6:24 (NIV)

"Now by this we know that we know Him, if we keep His commandments. He who says, 'I know Him,' and does not keep His commandments, is a liar, and the truth is not in him. But whoever keeps His word, truly the love of God is perfected in him. By this we know that we are in Him. He who says he abides in Him ought himself also to walk just as He walked." —1 John 2:3-6 (NKJV)

" 'If my people, who are called by my name, will humble themselves and pray and seek my face and turn from their wicked ways, then will I hear from heaven and will forgive their sin and will heal their land.' " —2 Chronicles 7:14 (NIV)

"If we confess our sins, he is faithful and just to forgive us our sins, and to cleanse us from all unrighteousness." —1 John 1:9 (KJV)

" 'Whoever has my commands and obeys them, he is the one who loves me. He who loves me will be loved by my Father, and I too will love him and show myself to him.' " —John 14:21 (NIV)

the people

When they saw it, they all murmured, saying, That he was gone to be guest with a man that is a sinner (Luke 19:7, KJV).

Zacchaeus was in for the surprise of his life. He had just met the One who would bring a powerful new dimension to his life. His burdens were lifted, his life was made new, his sins were forgiven, and a new peace permeated his entire soul. Yet, instead of hearing the shouts of hearty "Amen!" and "Praise the Lord!" to commemorate his birth into the kingdom of grace, Zacchaeus heard the careless and evil whispers of a critical and unbelieving crowd. Imagine: On the happiest day of his life, there were people at the scene whose only response was to sow seeds of negativity and contempt! "When they saw it, they all murmured."

New Loyalty, Old Tricks

Satan's schemes are always impeccably designed and timed to cause the maximum amount of damage to anyone who decides to follow God. He succeeds most often by using people who can't recognize when God is at work. And if he fails at using people to block your view so that you can't see the Lord fully, he'll attempt to use people to discourage you after you've had an undeniable encounter with God.

Notice that as soon as Zacchaeus shifted his loyalty to Christ by obeying the command to come down out of the tree, the evil one began throwing his darts to pierce deeply into his newly found faith. Now, let it be known that Zacchaeus was not born yesterday. He was not naïve to the fickle and sometimes cruel ways of people. Matter of fact, he had grown numb from taking verbal beatings from people who didn't truly know him. However, he thought this crowd would be different. These were people who followed the Master. These were the ones who were in Christ's presence as He performed miracles and healings. These were the folks

the zacchaeus effect

who sat attentively at His feet while words of life flowed from holy lips. These people were supposed to be ... different.

Let me make two statements that may help us place the people we encounter in their proper perspective. First, we cannot always gauge the quality of our choices by the response of the majority, especially when it comes to choices that have moral and eternal significance and consequences.

1. Martin Luther was excommunicated from the church for taking an unpopular (biblical) position that the "just shall live by faith."

2. Shadrach, Meshach, and Abednego were sentenced to die because they were the only ones in the crowd who chose not to bow down to a false god.

3. Nelson Mandela suffered for twenty-seven years in prison because he took a stand against a whole nation that embraced the evil system of apartheid.

4. Harriet Tubman was labeled a fugitive and a criminal for helping to lead slaves to freedom through the ingenious Underground Railroad.

5. Noah was mocked, scorned, and derided by all humanity for building an ark and for preaching a

message that ultimately would be believed by only his own family.

6. Jesus dared to save humankind by showing unselfish love; but He was castigated, convicted, and crucified on a cross by an angry, bloodthirsty mob.

Simply put, crowds can be wrong. The majority can make mistakes. Church folks are not always right. And frankly, taking a courageous and unpopular stand for the Lord can be a scary thing to do. Yet our only safety is found in faithfully listening to and following the voice of the One whose will and ways are perfect.

Second, there is no guarantee that the crowd that hangs around God will always behave in a godly manner. Joining the family of God does not inoculate you from unfair, undeserved, and sometimes unkind words or treatment. Nor does it shield you from behavior that maybe you were accustomed to seeing in the world. The reality is that people who wear the name of Christ are not always kind and pleasant. Many are growing and immature. Others may have years in membership yet still be neophytes in discipleship. Some may be downright unconverted.

Sometimes even those who are supposed to be closest to Christ will be used as agents of vicious gossip and tools of discouragement. A line from an old Negro spiritual puts it best: "Ev'rybody talkin' 'bout heav'n ain't goin' there." Satan will make sure that there will be a little bit of everything in the household of faith to distract and halt your progress.

Momentarily stunned, wounded by the arrows of unholy conversations and satanic attacks, Zacchaeus had to quickly refocus on the one thing that counted—the promise of the Lord's presence: "Today I must *abide* at your house." He chose to listen to the promise of Jesus above the noise of the critics and naysayers. In doing so, he discovered that the only realm where true peace is found is in the awesome Word of God.

Get this in your spirit: Never allow words to overshadow the Word. His Word is always true. The sooner you learn this, the better off you will be in your walk with God. And before you know it, you will be home.

Reflecting on the WORD

Read and reflect on each text to discover the necessity of possessing endurance and peace even while being tested and tried by evil and evildoers.

"Do not be anxious about anything, but in everything, by prayer and petition, with thanksgiving, present your requests to God. And the peace of God, which transcends all understanding, will guard your hearts and your minds in Christ Jesus. Finally, brothers, whatever is true, whatever is noble, whatever is right, whatever is pure, whatever is lovely, whatever is admirable—if anything is excellent or praiseworthy— think about such things. Whatever you have learned or received or heard from me, or seen in me—put it into practice. And the God of peace will be with you."
—Philippians 4:6-9 (NIV)

"Dear friends, do not be surprised at the painful trial you are suffering, as though something strange were happening to you. But rejoice that you participate in the sufferings of Christ, so that you may be overjoyed when his glory is revealed. If you are insulted because of the name of Christ, you are blessed, for the Spirit of glory and of God rests on you." —1 Peter 4:12-14 (NIV)

" 'Blessed are those who are persecuted because of righteousness, for theirs is the kingdom of heaven. Blessed are you when people insult you, persecute you and falsely say all kinds of evil against you because of me. Rejoice and be glad, because great is your reward in heaven, for in the same way they persecuted the prophets who were before you....

But I tell you: Love your enemies and pray for those who persecute you.' " —Matthew 5:10-12, 44 (NIV)

"Be strong in the Lord and in his mighty power. Put on the full armor of God so that you can take your stand against the devil's schemes. For our struggle is not against flesh and blood, but against the rulers, against the authorities, against the powers of this dark world and against the spiritual forces of evil in the heavenly realms. Therefore put on the full armor of God, so that when the day of evil comes, you may be able to stand your ground, and after you have done everything, to stand." —Ephesians 6:10-13 (NIV)

CHAPTER 10

the proof

Zacchaeus stood, and said unto the Lord; Behold, Lord, the half of my goods I give to the poor; and if I have taken any thing from any man by false accusation, I restore him fourfold (Luke 19:8, KJV).

Let me attempt to clear up something that may be helpful to someone. To *confess* our sins is not the same as to *repent* of them. Confession involves one saying or agreeing with God that what has been done—the sinful choice, thought, action, or behavior—is indeed sin, and one is forthcoming in declaring or calling it by its right name: *sin*. Not a *mistake* or *error* or just *having fun* or an *alternative lifestyle*, but *sin*. It is agreeing with what God has already declared it to be. It is an honest attempt not to sugarcoat or to gloss over the enormity of sin.

Repentance, on the other hand, involves not only agreeing and declaring that sin is sin, but determining to change the behavior. Repentance says that not only have our minds changed about the sin, but also that we will no longer walk in that direction. There is a complete turnaround. Because your mind has been changed, your actions will follow.

I have preached many sermons over the years. One of the frustrations of declaring God's Word is that many do not take it as a blueprint for modern living. I have arrived at the point in ministry where it is not enough for me to hear applause, excitement, or enthusiasm about God's Word. My greatest thrill comes when someone decides to apply God's Word in order to change his or her conduct. Too many times we get excited about revelation but fall short when it comes to application.

Notice that the first thing Zacchaeus did after obeying God was stand up: "Zacchaeus stood …" Sin causes you to bend over and be weighed down and fall. It causes guilt and a troubled mind. But when Jesus touched Zacchaeus with His power and freed him from his sins, Zacchaeus straightened up his back and squared his shoulders and stood tall. No more burdens, no more deceit, no more lies. Zacchaeus was free.

Then came the real proof of his conversion. Unfortunately, many in the household of faith have learned how to stand and pray and even look holy in God's presence, but in reality there is no difference in the heart. There is no authentic change. Zacchaeus did more than just look different—he *was* different: "Behold, Lord, the half of my goods I give to the poor; and if I have taken any thing from any man by false accusation, I restore him fourfold."

A Story to Remember

In the summer of 1991, I had the privilege of conducting an old-fashioned tent revival in the city of Compton, California. Being young and full of energy, I launched out into a public evangelistic campaign that would last for several weeks. To advertise these services, we printed banners, posters, and handbills that were hung and distributed all over the town. Included on these advertising pieces were the topics of the messages that I would present each evening.

I first encountered Ray while he was staring at one of the posters hanging on a telephone pole outside the tent. After approaching him, I introduced myself and gave him a personal invitation to attend one of the services. He smiled and asked, "Are you actually going to preach on a *different* subject each night for all the weeks of the revival?" I responded that I would do the very best I could. Looking surprised and slightly impressed at how a young man could have so much knowledge (I was still in my twenties), he promised that he would attend at least one of the meetings.

The next evening Ray came. After the service, I greeted him and thanked him for attending. I asked him if the sermon was clear and then ventured to ask his opinion about the content of the message. He shared with me some honest feedback and concluded that he generally "got something out of it" and planned to come back again. Impressed by his candid yet insightful response, I thanked him and told him that I was looking forward to his return. Truthfully, I do not know how it came to be, but a special bond between a young preacher and another one of God's prodigals began that night.

I imagine the ones who were observing this budding friendship didn't quite know what to make of it, because, on the surface, it seemed that we were mismatched. Make no mistake about it: Ray was a tough cookie. He smoked. He drank. He occasionally used drugs. His language was occasionally too "spicy" for the saints. He had served time in prison. And to top it off, he walked around rarely smiling while wearing dark sunglasses. But despite all the stuff that I was learning about Ray that might have driven away some of the more "blueblooded" saints, I actually *liked* him.

To put it more bluntly, the more time I spent with him, the more I realized how alike we were at the core: Ray had earned a four-year college degree, he loved his family dearly, and he was extremely intelligent (well, there go the similarities) and intensely loyal. More importantly, however, he had a heart of gold. Unfortunately, he had made some choices in his life that he was paying dearly for. Yet hidden just a few inches below his hardened exterior, Ray was one of the nicest people that I had ever met. Our habits may have been different, but our condition was the same: SINNER. I was only, as D. T. Niles said, "one beggar telling another beggar where to find some bread."

Let me caution people who may have the tendency to turn up their noses at people who may look or act a little differently from you: Never judge a book by its cover. Never. Hidden below the surface there is often a new person screaming to get out. Do not forget this: Just as God has graciously died for you, He has died for others. His blood can cover any sin, background, mistake, crime, or lifestyle. Just as sure as God has a plan for you, He has a plan for all His creation.

Well, back to the story of my friend. During the crusade, God touched the heart of Ray and began to change his life. He confessed his sins and was baptized as a public declaration of his serious decision to begin a new life with Jesus as his personal Savior and Lord. Immediately God began to work out the wrinkles of his life. A few months later the Lord gave him a spouse, who was instrumental in praying with Ray while he was making the divine transition and who was also part of the crusade team as a Bible counselor. (By the way, their first "date" took place in my home—now, tell me that God isn't good!)

I am glad to report that even though more than a decade has passed, Ray and his wife are still passionately in love with the Lord and with each other. They share in ministry together (both are ordained elders in their local church), and Ray is experiencing success both professionally and financially. His lifestyle has totally changed; he is enjoying the benefits of living the sanctified life. But best of all, he has become one the greatest friends that God has ever given me, and we now enjoy watching each other grow as we both strive to follow the path that God has planned for our lives.

The proof of an authentic encounter with Jesus is a changed life. That which had possessed Zacchaeus for so many years no longer had a hold on him. The name, money, prestige, and material possessions did not matter to him anymore. He had found a joy that he could not describe. He wanted everyone to know that he had met a Man who had completely altered his values and reoriented his personality. He was truly "born again." Confession gave way to repentance, and Zacchaeus became Exhibit A in the case of the transforming power of God.

Remember this: If you've really encountered the Savior, you will automatically change your behavior. I'm not speaking of perfection but of your direction! I guess the old people in my church community said it best while I was growing up: "If you've truly been born again, you ought to show some sign."

So stand up and let His goodness shine through you today. It will really be the beginning of the best part of your life!

Reflecting on the WORD

Read each text and think on the power of God to change lives completely and fully. If you already know the Lord, have you allowed the Lord to transform your entire life for His glory?

"If anyone is in Christ, he is a new creation; old things have passed away; behold, all things have become new." —2 Corinthians 5:17 (NKJV)

"We were therefore buried with him through baptism into death in order that, just as Christ was raised from the dead through the glory of the Father, we too may live a new life. If we have been united with him like this in his death, we will certainly also be united with him in his resurrection. For we know that our old self was crucified with him so that the body of sin might be done away with, that we should no longer be slaves to sin—because anyone who has died has been freed from sin. Now if we died with Christ, we believe that we will also live with him." —Romans 6:4-8 (NIV)

"What happiness for those whose guilt has been forgiven! What joys when sins are covered over! What relief for those who have confessed their sins and God has cleared their record." —Psalm 32:1 (TLB)

"No one who is born of God will continue to sin, because God's seed remains in him; he cannot go on sinning, because he has been born of God. This is how we know who the children of God are and who the children of the devil are: Anyone who does not do what is right is not a child of God; nor is anyone who does not love his brother." —1 John 3:9, 10 (NIV)

"Being confident of this, that he who began a good work in you will carry it on to completion until the day of Christ Jesus." —Philippians 1:6 (NIV)

"Whatsoever is born of God overcometh the world: and this is the victory that overcometh the world, even our faith." —1 John 5:4 (KJV)

"Let them thank the Lord for his steadfast love, for his wonderful works to the sons of men! For he satisfies him who is thirsty, and the hungry he fills with good things." —Psalm 107:8, 9 (RSV)

the promise

Jesus said unto him, This day is salvation come to this house
(Luke 19:9, KJV).

To Zacchaeus, these words of Jesus must have seemed like a cool drink of water on a hot summer day. After all the guilt, apprehension, waiting, wondering, and confessing, the Lord spoke a powerful promise: "*Today*, salvation has arrived at your house" (Luke 19:9; Peeler's Revised Version).

Notice that this liberating and comforting promise of assurance came to Zacchaeus at the very moment he decided to let go control of his life. The promise came the very second Jesus perceived

Zacchaeus's inward posture of total surrender. The promise came when the Messiah observed that this unfulfilled tax collector would welcome Him to perform a surgery to completely revamp his value system. At the very point in time when Zacchaeus decided to leave the past behind and grab hold of the Lord of the future, the Word proclaimed a word. And the promise was clear, concise, and poignant: "This day salvation has come to your house!"

Frankly, I am disturbed by many well-meaning saints and scholars who have unfortunately made the understanding of this whole salvation issue a difficult thing. They teach a message that turns the gospel of grace into a bartering session with the Almighty in which we attempt to exchange our money or good deeds in return for His grace. I am equally appalled at the proponents of "cheap grace" who attempt to dilute the elements of sincerity and commitment that are absolutely necessary when one decides to move from darkness into light. Our salvation costs too much for us to make it a trite issue. We somehow need to learn to appreciate salvation's price without minimizing the gift.

Setting the Record Straight

Although in the previous chapter we discovered that Zacchaeus had an overwhelming urge to make up for his past by correcting any previous misdeeds, he may not have initially understood the true reason for his new motivation and desire to please the Lord. So, in addition to quieting the crowd by publicly declaring Zacchaeus's new position and standing within the kingdom of grace, I believe that the Lord also took this time to share with Zacchaeus the true nature of His gift. He made sure that Zacchaeus understood that he couldn't do anything to qualify for his salvation.

Therefore, after hearing the skepticism of the crowd and then observing the response of his newest disciple, Jesus felt compelled to set the record straight by explaining the futility of making any efforts to impress others or even Himself when it involved the issue of salvation. "Zacchaeus," He said, "as of this moment, salvation is already yours."

It is a sad commentary when those who have joined the body of Christ feel compelled to impress others with their newfound "spirituality" by doing good deeds and working hard. It's sadder still when people try to impress God by punching the clock of works in order to pay for something that God is offering for free. Satan is constantly misrepresenting God by making Him appear like a narcissistic deity who systematically demands deeds, money, and even praise in exchange for His love and salvation. Beware of this errant teaching. Personally, I have a one-word response to this incorrect and unbiblical conception of God: BOGUS! You can't save yourself anymore than you can change your height—just ask Zacchaeus! Salvation that comes from God is free, and it is based solely on His love for us—period!

Please do not misunderstand me on this point and reach an incorrect conclusion concerning the significance of obedience—a conclusion stating that once we have received the gift of salvation, our obedience to God no longer plays a factor in our lifestyle as believers. Indeed, it does. What I am laboring to make clear is that our obedience to our Lord is futile unless we have first received His salvation. Our obedience to Him should come only from the overflow of our love for Him that is based on a personal relationship.

Do me a favor and memorize this next statement; it may save you years of painstaking labor and sweat: One should never try to obey the Lord *to* be saved—we should only choose to obey Him *because* we are saved. Our only source of lasting power to obey is the strength that comes from abiding in the Lord. In *His* righteousness. In *His* power. In *His* salvation. So His promise is really a covenant declaring, "As long as I am with you and you are with Me, I will then give you the ability to do whatever I reveal to you." Encountering the Lord should always precede anything that we do for Him or for His cause.

If you are having a difficult time with this truism, notice again the timeframe of the promise: "Salvation is yours today!" Salvation was guaranteed on the very day of Zacchaeus's awesome encounter with grace. "This day" literally meant now! Right now! Right at this very moment—not *"after* you have shown yourself to be good enough"; not *"after* you have given all your money to charities"; not *"after* you have memorized the entire Bible"; not *"after* you start dressing or eating appropriately"; not *"after* you've learned to preach like Peter and pray like the apostle Paul." *"Today,* salvation is yours!" It is the immediate declaration of His justification to anyone who receives the gift of His forgiveness, cleansing, and regeneration.

I have been blessed to have parents who have modeled a consistent spirit of giving as long as I can remember. Though far from being wealthy, they always opened our home to friends, relatives, and just about anyone who needed help. Throughout my childhood, I witnessed how they unselfishly and faithfully gave back to the Lord and then to others.

Several years back I planned a short trip to visit my parents. As I was preparing to leave, I received news of a friend on the East Coast whose wife had suddenly died, and he was in desperate need of help with the expenses for the funeral. Though my wife and I were not in the most comfortable position to give a lot of money at that time, the Lord convinced us to send money to help instead of using money to fly to the services. Once this assignment was handled, I continued with my plans by catching a flight to visit my folks.

I was extremely glad to have helped out my friend in crisis. I would be hypocritical, however, if I did not admit that I secretly wondered how we were going to pay the bills that the money was originally intended for. I even started thinking of doing some extra work to make up the difference.

After spending a few enjoyable days relaxing and reminiscing at the place of my youth, I quickly packed my bags to catch my flight back home. While packing, I noticed an envelope with my name on it that lay on the bed. I figured it was something that I could read later, so I stuffed it in my bag, and, quite honestly, forgot about it. A few days later my mother called to see how I was doing, but more specifically, to inquire about the envelope she had left.

I informed her that I had been so busy that I hadn't opened it. Being the mom she is, she told me, "Well, find it and open it!" I gulped hard, because it reminded me of her tone when she used to warm my seat as a child.

It took only a few moments to locate the envelope in my still-unpacked bag. Lo and behold, without knowing what we had given to our friend in need, my mother had been impressed to give me the exact same amount—several hundred dollars. When I called her back, she explained to me that, as a recently retired school nurse, she received an unexpected blessing in the form of a check in the mail, and, after returning her tithes and offering to the Lord, she was moved to pass her blessing on to her grown children.

My first response was, "Mom, I'll pay it back when I get the money." She sternly replied, "Boy, don't be silly! That money is yours. I gave it as a gift. Just take it and use it as you see fit. Take it, and, when you can, pass the blessing along. But remember, you don't owe me a thing." Thankful, yet humbled, I received the gift that came from the hand of God but through the heart of my mother.

Even now, after all these years, she and my Pop continue to show their love by committing to give their best to their children … and grandchildren … and now, even to their great-grandchild. To me, that is mind-blowing.

The promise Zacchaeus received that day was a gift that included instant salvation. The Lord still dispenses promises we can count on and packages that contain limitless doses of eternal life through His blood. His only condition is that we must not try to pay for it with our money, influence, or good works—for His gift of salvation is absolutely free. So don't forget; it's that simple. Now, all you have to do is receive it, and, when you can, pass the blessing along!

Reflecting on the WORD

Read each passage to get a picture of the precious gift of salvation that is offered to everyone who sincerely desires it. Based on these texts, can we do anything to earn our salvation?

"God, being rich in mercy, because of His great love with which He loved us, even when we were dead in our transgressions, made us alive together with Christ (by grace you have been saved), and raised us up with Him, and seated us with Him in the heavenly places, in Christ Jesus, in order that in the ages to come He might show the surpassing riches of His grace in kindness toward us in Christ Jesus. For by grace you have been saved through faith; and that not of yourselves, it is the gift of God; not as a result of works, that no one should boast. For we are His workmanship, created in Christ Jesus for good works, which God prepared beforehand, that we should walk in them." —Ephesians 2:4-10 (NAS)

"When the kindness of God our Savior and His love for mankind appeared, He saved us, not on the basis of deeds which we have done in righteousness, but according to His mercy, by the washing of regeneration and renewing by the Holy Spirit, whom He poured out upon us richly through Jesus Christ our Savior, that being justified by His grace we might be made heirs according to the hope of eternal life." —Titus 3:4-7 (NAS)

"Do not be ashamed of the testimony of our Lord or of me His prisoner; but join with me in suffering for the gospel according to the power of God; who has saved us, and called us with a holy calling, not according to our works, but according to His own purpose and grace which was granted us in Christ Jesus from all eternity." — 2 Timothy 1:8, 9 (NAS)

"If thou shalt confess with thy mouth the Lord Jesus, and shalt believe in thine heart that God hath raised him from the dead, thou shalt be saved. For with the heart man believeth unto righteousness; and with the mouth confession is made unto salvation." —Romans 10:9,10 (KJV)

"If any man is in Christ, he is a new creature; the old things passed away; behold, new things have come.

Now all these things are from God, who reconciled us to Himself through Christ, and gave us the ministry of reconciliation, namely, that God was in Christ reconciling the world to Himself, not counting their trespasses against them, and He has committed to us the word of reconciliation. Therefore, we are ambassadors for Christ, as though God were entreating through us; we beg you on behalf of Christ, be reconciled to God. He made Him who knew no sin to be sin on our behalf, that we might become the righteousness of God in Him." —2 Corinthians 5:17-21 (NAS)

CHAPTER 12

the privilege

Jesus said unto him, This day is salvation come to this house, forsomuch as he also is a son of Abraham (Luke 19:9, KJV).

Many years ago while I was in college, I met someone whom I was determined to know. There was something about her that made me interested, and although I could not say exactly what it was, something inside me lit up every time I saw her walking across campus. Whenever I was in her presence, I would make certain that I struck up a conversation with her, and soon we became friends.

Our friendship grew into love, and that love grew into commitment, which grew into marriage. Reflecting back on more than twenty-two years of knowing her, all I can write is that God has truly smiled on me by giving me my wife, Brenda. She is a beautiful woman, a committed wife, a wonderful mother of our three daughters, a gifted professional, and most of all, a spirit-filled Christian. (I guess she *has* to be since she's put up with me this long!) And it all began because I wanted to know her.

What continues to astound me is the *way* that she loves me even after getting to know the *real* me! Though she recognizes that I am far from being perfect, she continues to shower me with unconditional love and genuinely takes pride in all the achievements that God has allowed me to enjoy.

Throughout our marriage, I've also been privileged to be the recipient of letters from her expressing her love and appreciation for me. I'll allow you to read one of her notes that I keep posted over my desk in my home office:

> *It seems as though we just met, for I cannot believe that you captured my heart ten years ago! So much has happened since we first met. I can remember the first time I saw you on the*

campus of La Sierra. My first impression of you was positive. It didn't take long for our friendship to develop. I remember those long talks that we would have (usually with you attempting to ask me out at some point during the conversation); but more than anything, I always felt that you were a true friend. There was no pressure in our friendship. Instead, we were just two people who enjoyed each other's company.

The foundation of friendship that we developed early in our relationship, I believe, is one of the things that has kept our marriage strong. I count it a true blessing to be able to say that I am married to a man that I consider to be spiritual, compassionate, handsome, sexy, fun, bright, talented, resourceful, nurturing, and all that!

The words "I Love You" really do not express all of the meaning that I want to express to you; but I hope that with each passing day as we share our life together, I can help you to know that each time I look in your eyes, see your smile, hear your voice, and feel your touch, my love for you grows.

*Emil Dean Peeler, I recommit my love to you
this 19th day of August 1994.
Forever yours,
Brenda*

The Greatest Love We'll Ever Know

That's an amazing kind of love, isn't it? Now sit back and imagine this: God's love for us far exceeds any love that can exist on a human level. In fact, He is love! No matter what we have done in the past, He loves us with an everlasting love, and He desires a deep and abiding relationship with *us*. His entire purpose for coming to this earth was to give His love and life to all who desire it.

Let me note two characteristics that I believe are worth sharing about God's love. First of all, His love is unconditional. That simply means that He loves us with a love that knows no boundary or limit. It is a love that is pure, holy, and simply awesome, and the depth of His love is not based on our deeds, behavior, attitudes, or even our response to *His* love and blessings. He doesn't calculate how many sins we've committed before He dispenses His mercy. Matter of fact, He already knows all our thoughts, motives, failings, and secret desires—

the *real* us—and yet He keeps loving us anyway!

Before you shake your head in disbelief, let me hurry to the next thing that you should know right away about God's love: It's truly inexplicable! That means it is beyond our comprehension. Try as we may, we humans cannot ascertain or adequately put in words that which is truly indescribable. His love is so deep and vast that

Shakespeare can't describe it!

Speech can't express it!

Nouns can't name it!

Water can't drown it!

Scales can't weigh it!

Fire can't burn it!

Art can't portray it!

Psychology can't understand it!

Logic can't reason it!

Science can't discover it!

Adjectives can't describe it!

Bill Gates can't buy it!

I am speaking of true, unconditional, unchanging, unwavering, indescribable, incomprehensible love, which only God can give. Forget about the sentimental love that we see plastered on the big screen.

Away with the kind of love that rises and falls based on the tide of one's emotions. God's love is far above and beyond anything that we can ever think or imagine." 'The Son of man came to seek and to save the lost' " (Luke 19:10, RSV). Get this—He has even written sixty-six love letters with our name and address all over them! And each of these letters describes various aspects of His love for us. I know it seems impossible, but it's true.

Like Zacchaeus, you may have been looking for love in all the wrong places. I dare you to open up wide your heart and eyes to the Truth, and you will discover true Love coming down the road toward your house.

Reflecting on the WORD

Read these passages and then take time to reflect on how wonderful it is for us to have the privilege of unconditional love from a holy and perfect God.

"Dear friends, let us love one another, for love comes from God. Everyone who loves has been born of God and knows God. Whoever does not love does not know God, because God is love. This is how God showed his love among us: He sent his one and only

Son into the world that we might live through him. This is love: not that we loved God, but that he loved us and sent his Son as an atoning sacrifice for our sins. Dear friends, since God so loved us, we also ought to love one another. No one has ever seen God; but if we love one another, God lives in us and his love is made complete in us." —1 John 4:7-12 (NIV)

"Christ may dwell in your hearts through faith. And I pray that you, being rooted and established in love, may have power, together with all the saints, to grasp how wide and long and high and deep is the love of Christ, and to know this love that surpasses knowledge—that you may be filled to the measure of all the fullness of God." —Ephesians 3:17-19 (NIV)

"Who shall separate us from the love of Christ? Shall trouble or hardship or persecution or famine or nakedness or danger or sword? As it is written: 'For your sake we face death all day long; we are considered as sheep to be slaughtered.' No, in all these things we are more than conquerors through him who loved us. For I am convinced that neither death nor life, neither angels nor demons, neither the present nor the future, nor any powers, neither height nor depth, nor anything else in all creation, will be able to separate us from the love of God that is in Christ Jesus our Lord." —Romans 8:35-39 (NIV)

"The mountains shall depart, and the hills be removed; but my kindness shall not depart from thee, neither shall the covenant of my peace be removed, saith the Lord that hath mercy on thee." —Isaiah 54:10 (KJV)

"May our Lord Jesus Christ himself and God our Father, who loved us and by his grace gave us eternal encouragement and good hope, encourage your hearts and strengthen you in every good deed and word." —2 Thessalonians 2:16, 17 (NIV)

CHAPTER 13

the person

*The Son of man is come to seek and to save that which was lost
(Luke 19:10, KJV).*

As a boy growing up in Sacramento, California, I took great delight in playing with my older brothers, Marcus and Barron, along with a host of neighborhood kids. During those days, there were no PlayStations, Game Boys, or Nintendos. Instead, we spent our recreational time in the outdoors playing some sports: basketball, baseball, football. We raced, skated, and even tried boxing. Usually, as we played, we all pretended to be our favorite professional athlete from the sport that we happened to be playing at the moment. I had many sports idols: Willie Mays, Kareem Abdul-Jabbar, Kenny Stabler, and many others.

However, I must confess that no athlete captivated my attention more than "The Greatest," Muhammad Ali. Make no mistake about it: I *loved* that guy. I filled my room with his posters, I memorized his poems, I knew all his fight record—I literally studied every detail about his life. I watched all his fights that were on television, and when they were broadcast on closed-circuit television (nowadays called pay-per-view), I simply tuned in on the radio to hear the summary of each round. When he won, I felt I had won also. I was his greatest fan . . . because he was *the man!*

I wish that I could report that my adoration of Ali tapered off by the time I reached college, but it didn't. I had it bad! Then one day, it happened: He was scheduled to speak at a place only an hour's drive away. I *had* to see him up close and personal, in flesh and blood. So I arrived at the place and took my seat—and to my absolute delight, there he was: tall, handsome, winsome—"The Greatest!"

I can't remember much of what Muhammad Ali spoke about that evening, but I certainly do recall that

I wasn't going to miss out on this once in-a-lifetime chance of at least touching his hand. At the conclusion of the program, I raced outside to where his waiting Rolls Royce was parked. People crowded around him as he slowly made his way to the open door awaiting him. For a moment I thought that I wouldn't get the chance to shake his hand. Then, as he was about to arrive at his vehicle, I loudly called out his name to get his attention. He stopped, then turned around, and our eyes met. I lunged forward in a desperate attempt to reach and touch his hand. Remarkably, he smiled and reached back through the crowd to grab my hand, and we touched. I literally thought that I had died and gone to heaven! I was euphoric because I had finally touched the hand of my hero, one who was considered by many to be the greatest fighter who ever lived.

I went back to my dormitory and told everyone I saw about this watershed event in my life. Some pretended to be excited with me, but most people just looked blankly at me as if to say, "So, what's the big deal?" I remained undaunted by their reactions, however, for I was determined not to let anyone take my moment of glory from me.

A Lesson Learned

Later that night, God allowed me to learn a powerful lesson. As I was basking in the glow of the evening, something dawned on me. I had *touched* the hand of a famous man, but nothing about my life actually changed. I still had bills, work, school, and a host of other responsibilities. I was in the exact same state that I was in before I made contact with "The Greatest." Emptiness still pervaded my heart. I had discovered that a person's deepest longings of the soul can never be fully satisfied by other people, by possessions, by power, or by the pursuit of pleasure. Let me emphasize this fact: *Never!*

Let's get real. Despite the enemy's universal advertising campaign to the contrary, the facts are that the fickle bubble of pleasure does not last; the empty husks of amusement will never satisfy the longing of a hurting, shallow soul; the pursuit of fortune and fame is an endless, tiresome journey to a hollow existence; getting drunk and high and having lots of sexual partners is not only dangerous to your health, but also applies merely temporary bandages that inadequately cover up the cancerous erosion of an unrenewed heart; and even a life full of good deeds and charitable works will not guarantee ultimate fulfillment. In the course of time, people get old and die, material things lose their luster, the titillating lure of the "good life" erodes, and power fades away. It is as simple as that. Things of this earth do not last! The Bible is clear that the pleasures of sin are only for a season (see Hebrews 11:25).

Let me hasten to report the best part of the story. A few short years later, there came a moment when I decided to climb up my "tree" and truly listen to the unmistakable voice of a Person who had called me since my birth. It was a night that I will never forget. During a week of spiritual emphasis, a young preacher named Walter Pearson came to the campus where I was attending college at the time. The spiritual atmosphere in that church was electric. Each evening, I found myself rushing to get a seat to hear a word from the Lord. Pearson's preaching was powerful, biblical, and practical. And then … it happened! While the preacher was passionately describing the Lord dying on His tree, I had a personal encounter with the Lord. I truly *saw* Jesus for myself.

No doubt there were many instances before this moment when I had glanced casually at Jesus. I had viewed Him in the lives of my godly parents, and in the lives of preachers and saints in the church where I grew up. I had seen Him work in my life as a protector and deliverer when the enemy had unsuccessfully tried to snuff out my existence. I had heard countless sermons. I had faithfully gone to church and even learned songs about Him. I was actually really well acquainted with Him. But, until that moment in the fall of 1981, I had never taken the time to gaze into His glorious face, to really desire to *know* Him intimately.

Looking back, I now realize that it was God who had patiently stood with me through all of my issues, mistakes, and rebellion to orchestrate that particular moment in time. That night I saw Jesus, and hot tears of repentance and joy streamed down my face. Jesus reached out to me and touched me with His presence, power, and peace. And I must say that since that day I have never been the same.

Bill and Gloria Gaither wrote of that kind of experience in their classic song, "He Touched Me." Guilt and shame weighed heavily upon the sinner, until "the hand of Jesus touched me—and now I am no longer the same."

That touch brings freedom. It releases the sinner from crippling guilt and shame. But more than that even, it brings joy—the joy that comes from being loved supremely!

This book is all about a Person—Jesus Christ. He is the only One who was willing to die while hanging on a tree in order that one day we would have a chance of finding Him while hanging from the branches of our own trees. And get this: He would have done it even if you or I had been the only person on earth!

So right now, I invite you to do yourself a favor: Find your tree and take a climb up it and take a look at His face. I know it may make you feel a little uncomfortable. The people around you may stop and stare and may even question your sanity. But take it from me—this will be one climb that will make all the difference in your world.

Don't misunderstand me. I am not inviting you to a life that will not have any challenges or obstacles; I would be remiss if I misrepresented what the Christian journey is all about. The truth is, the moment you decide to make this climb, all hell will literally break loose to try to shake you into believing that knowing God is not worth the struggle. Like Zacchaeus, on your way to your personal discovery of God, you may have to

1. Deal with people who block your view of the Almighty.
2. Come to grips with some of your own faults and shortcomings.
3. Learn to decipher the truth about God.
4. Leave some things and people behind in order to get ahead.
5. Stop making excuses for your present plight.
6. Be misunderstood and become the victim of stinging gossip.
7. Learn to choose righteousness over majority opinions.
8. Be constantly hassled by satanic emissaries.

To put it bluntly, it takes guts to *want* to get to know Jesus! For Zacchaeus, forming a true and lasting relationship with the Lord began with a mindset that was focused and resolute. Seeing the Lord that day was not an option—it was something he had to do. Some may call it a "made-up mind." This point is very important to grasp because our *actions* always follow our *thoughts*. Our behavior is a byproduct of what has been birthed in our minds.

Given this truism, you can either decide now to take the first step toward the Master or you can choose to continue to live a life of mediocrity that is destitute of His divine privileges. It's totally up to you. As your friend, however, let me be quick to say that if you choose God, I guarantee it will be the best choice of your life. Because what God has in store for your life is far greater than what you could ever imagine.

As I stated in chapter 1 of this volume, God has a plan for you—a divine scheme for your existence, a holy blueprint for your life. Not just for your family or your church or your country, but for you! You may not know it, understand it, or have accepted it, but His plan is there. It is intentional. Out of the billions of people who have lived and died on this earth, you've been chosen. GOD wants to be involved in a relationship with *you*.

I realize that this may be a bit much to swallow. The cynic in you may prefer to deny the truth of such a claim. But the fact of the matter remains: It's true. The Creator yearns for your friendship.

Like Zacchaeus, and countless other thankful saints, I have discovered that Jesus not only offers us

His friendship, but also the best deal in the universe: We give Him our sins, and He gives His forgiveness; we trade our sorrow for His joy, our confusion for His peace, and our past for His future. Awesome, isn't it?

I believe I've done enough small talk. Let's get down to business. Are you tired of your present predicament? Are your sins weighing you down? Are you unsatisfied with life? Do you need a change of pace? Are you swamped in guilt and self-pity? Do you desire a new start? Do you feel that you've blown it? Has the enemy convinced you that you've gone too far? Well, if you answered Yes to any of the above questions and are willing to move forward in faith, I have good news for you: Jesus is still able, willing, and available to turn your life around. Hallelujah!

Believe it or not, there is even a great possibility that He has orchestrated this moment for you to see Him. C'mon—don't wait any longer. Just pray this simple prayer:

Father,

Thank You for Your love and patience toward me. I have tried many things to fill my emptiness, but now I recognize that I am lost and incomplete without Your love, grace, and power. I confess and repent of the sins that have kept me from seeing Your love in my life. I now accept Your gift of salvation and pledge to listen to and obey Your Word by the power of Your Spirit until You return. Help me to live my life so that others can see You shining through me. Thank You so much for being my Savior, Lord, and Friend.

In the name of Jesus,
Amen.

One more thing. Since I met "The Greatest," my need for human idols has all but gone away. I figure, "Why settle for less when you have the Best?"

Still looking for a hero? Well, don't look any further—Jesus is all you will ever need!